A Life *of* Style

REBECCA MOSES

A Life *of* Style

Fashion • Home • Entertaining

The Monacelli Press

WHAT IS
THIS THING
CALLED
STYLE?
12

CONTENTS

WHAT IS A
LOOK?
46

WHAT
DEFINES A
HOME?
96

HOW ARE
MEMORIES
MADE?
166

To Giacomo,

love of my life, best friend, great father, and master of style.

Your spirit lives on.

And to our amazing children,

Virginia, Maximilian, and Benjamin, who fuel my creative energies.

You are the greatest gift your father ever gave me.

I must begin by acknowledging my husband Giacomo, who passed away just as this book went to press. Giacomo showed me how to truly live the sweet life that Italians cherish and shared with me the joy of opening our home to our eclectic family and friends.

My sister, Deborah, my alter ego, encouraged me to embark on this book. Her relentless belief that I could do it kept it alive through many challenging moments.

I am grateful to my parents, Barbara and Howard, who gave me the confidence to live my dreams, and to my Italian family, my in-laws Piera and Ottavio Festa Bianchet. I could not have asked for more wonderful people to teach me the Italian culture.

There have been special women and men whose spirit touched my life and influenced me, who have been cherished friends and mentors, who are themselves true style visionaries: Donatella Girombelli; Joyce Ma; Bonnie Gokson; Dawn Mello; Vera Wang; Nicole Fischelis; Bridget Foley, Etta Froio, and Alessandra Ilari; Freddie Leiba; and Donata Satoria.

There are simply not enough pages in this book to give my friends their due: Laura and Pigi Loro Piana, my greatest teachers in life, love, and the meaning of friendship; Alberto and Monica Illorinni, who shared with me twenty years of love, laughter, and wonder; Gianni and Maria Grazia Chiarva, who taught me the "no limits" concept of love, life, and extraordinary friendship; Eitan and Ariella Wertheimer; Antonella and Jack Moretti; Sergio and Luisa Loro Piana; Ubi and Tito Odero; Georgia and Ron Frasch; and of course Gruppo Vacanza, the crazy and loving group of friends who showed me how to live a stylish life on the sea and also the value of friendship.

I thank Larry Shatz of Grubman, Indursky & Schindler; Theresa Heiner; Sabrina Fung; Laura Romangnoli; Roberta Ciappi; Michelle Hillman; Lou Iacovelli; Graziella Gabban and Ilenia Ronchi; Stephanie Bridgestock; Stephano Marchetti; and Paola Ratazzi. Your hearts and passions enhance my life.

A special thank you to my licensing partner, Li & Fung USA, and Rick Darling, Mark Wolk, David Greenstein, and Allan Chartash, who have helped further my fashion and home businesses.

I offer my heartfelt gratitude to Anna Wintour, whose support and belief over the course of my career have given me the confidence to pursue my vision of a life of style.

Shelley Wanger helped me find the right road to publish this book and became a dear friend in the process.

My publisher, Gianfranco Monacelli, a man of grace, wisdom, and vision, brought this project to fruition exactly as I dreamed it would be. Andrea Monfried, my editor, got to the heart of what is important. Icarus Leung brought his amazing talent and passion for typography to the art direction of this book. My agent, Jill Cohen, helped me understand that illustration is my voice. Sometimes the creative process can be over-whelming; she helped me find the way.

After three decades in the fashion business, I needed to stop and understand why and how this thing called style has ruled my life with such tenacity. I live to design and create. But for me, designing goes beyond the actual design. I think of the world around the design—the environment, mood, ambience, emotion, and spirit—as attached to the creative process. I have always asked myself, How do we live with design? How does design affect our lives? How do the clothes we wear, the homes we choose, the objects of our life communicate to the world who we are? I think of the way we live not as lifestyle but as a life *of style*. And to think in these terms you can't just look at the outside of style—you need to look at the inside of style. You need to understand the origins of how our style is derived, to appreciate why we love what we love.

And so I decided to put pen (and brush) to paper and start my own *style journey*. I needed to reflect on the source of all this love and passion. What made me develop into the person I am? How did my style evolve? Is style genetic, cultural, or life experience? I wanted to understand what my style DNA consisted of.

Was it Grandma Fanny's plastic-slipcovered King Louis sofa? My mother's forever un-matching chairs—and the incredible generosity in her home? Maybe a lifetime of old Hollywood films? My father, "the Cowboy"? Perhaps my first trip to Paris to meet Pierre Cardin? My first fashion show in Milan? My lavender bedroom in Secaucus? My first pair of hot pants? (Mom bought them at Bloomie's.) Capri? The Catskills?

The answer to this very loaded question is all of the above and much, much more. Style is a reflection of who we are, where we come from, and what we have experienced—the good, the bad, and the indifferent. It is what makes us into the unique beings that we are.

Having the courage to ask ourselves what we love *and why* is to really begin the process of understanding our style and enhancing the way we live and communicate who we are to the world around us.

Living a stylish life is not about buying designer clothes or retaining the "it" decorator of the moment. Nor is it about money. To live a life of style is to live with love, to nourish the passion to dream, to keep the faith, and last, but certainly not least, to understand who we are and how to say it.

I hope the book you are about to read will inspire you to live a life of style, to find the splendor and love of the world around you, and to understand yourself and the beautiful uniqueness that you have been born with. Life is a gift that we need to celebrate every day. Celebrate your life by living with love, passion, and *style*.

Rebecca Moses

START HERE...

My Style Journey

BORN WITH a desire to explore...

A few years later moved in with my Grandparents... I never understood why the King Louis sofa had transparent slip covers!! You could see the sofa, but just couldn't touch it. In the summer I would peel my legs off the sofa!

At five years my mother painted my room luscious lavender... a color that remained a signature my entire life...

My mother loved opening her house to everyone... She would just add tables, and the chairs never matched...

So natural... so much love and hospitality...

From 5 to 15 years I danced ballet with a lady named Jan Eyre. She was quite a striking lady, always in colorful leotards... She was very disciplined in dance and style...

Mom never left the house without her "face"!! Women always had their "face" on in public... I was always so proud when Mom came to school to speak to my teachers... To me she was the prettiest Mom.

In fact, Mom always went on Friday to the beauty parlor... it was a religion. Her hair was so high like the tower of Pisa... I never understood how she slept.

Daddy was honored by the Elks (a very 1960s American Club). Mom wore the most emerald green satin evening outfit... It was total Hollywood... She looked like a movie star!

Mom bought a crystal chandelier! It was so glamorous.

And then there was the Sonny and Cher Show!! Her clothes made me want to sketch!

My grandma worked in a beautiful hat shop... sold beautiful hats like the ones you could see in the movies... I love hats...

My mother and sister would watch old Hollywood movies on the Magnavox... The music, the dance, Grace, Fred, and Betty would make me dream of exotic places and high glamour...

We would go often to my grandma's house (my other grandma) and she had many beautiful pieces of furniture and the most wonderful wallpaper... My favorite chair was a wine satin wing chair...

MARRIAGE!! Giacomo + Rebecca

a family grows

MAX
BEN
VIRGI

New Friends + Family
Laura • Pigi.
Giami • MariGiorgia
Alberto • Monaco • Gitan
Piera • Ottavio
Arielle.

meet my American family and friends*

*Holidays in Capri • Monferatto
Portofino
Côte d'azur

Together we celebrate "la vera Dolce Vita" and a true "Life of Style!"

TIME FOR CHANGE

...e becomes GLOBAL!

...t Redefining cashmere

re-launch
REBECCA MOSES
Pineider

g
New design opportunities

It's the 90s a new decade, a new life... new everything...!
what a big change!

goodbye NYC.. hello Italy!

Could we have been more different?

2nd Divorce

New ♡ on its way

GIACOMO

new love
new Marriage...
new house, new everything
but... sometimes things don't go like you think!

...ngKong showed ...e..a grand over-the-top exotic ...yle...but more important ...ve me. friends for life...

My work in New York brings me to Asia and I meet Bonnie, Joyce, KT... it was wild, opulent; it was
HONG KONG

Deb (sister) Vera (friend)
model start doting, disco, designing. It was the 80's...

a crazier idea... my first marriage at 20 yrs.?!

PARIS! the Ritz!

DIVORCE 1 yr. later!

A crazy idea I'll start my own collection...

arrived on
SEVENTH AVE

My first job!!
Pierre Cardin
Coats Suits
18 yrs. old
and on my way to

My first Design on the cover of WWD!

WWD

2 years later

F.I.T

At 16 yrs. attended the Fashion Institute of Technology in NYC...

Old Hollywood Movies, Sonny and Cher, a glamorous Mom, and regular visits to Bloomie's made my Passion for fashion grow fast!

My favorite teenage fashion pieces

My Mom, sister, and I would go shopping at Bloomingdale's... In fact my father's request was to bury him at the entrance of Bloomie so that he would be sure we would visit regularly!

CLOGS

HOT PANTS

MAXI-COAT

Skinny Mini Sweaters

My father was and still is a cowboy... He grew up with horses and always wore a cowboy hat, Western style clothes, and cowboy boots. He is a + all man. Always stood out from the crowd ...He definitely had his "own" style...a bit over the top

Bloomingo

Bloomin

WHAT IS THIS THING CALLED STYLE?

The Key

to Style

Is there a key to style?

Or are there many keys?

How do we open the door to discover the style

that lies within us?

How do we unlock the honesty and desire

to tell the world who we are

and what we love and how we like to live

with what we love?

Some lucky individuals are born knowing what they love
and how they like to live.

This is innate style.

These people have a passion for appreciating everything
from the big picture to the fine details.
People with innate style put their stamp or signature
on everything they do: how they dress or decorate their
homes, dine, entertain, celebrate, relax, travel,
and conduct business and any other element of life,
from writing a note to planning a funeral.

These people are passionate about their style and the
way they live their style. They know how to
achieve what they want.

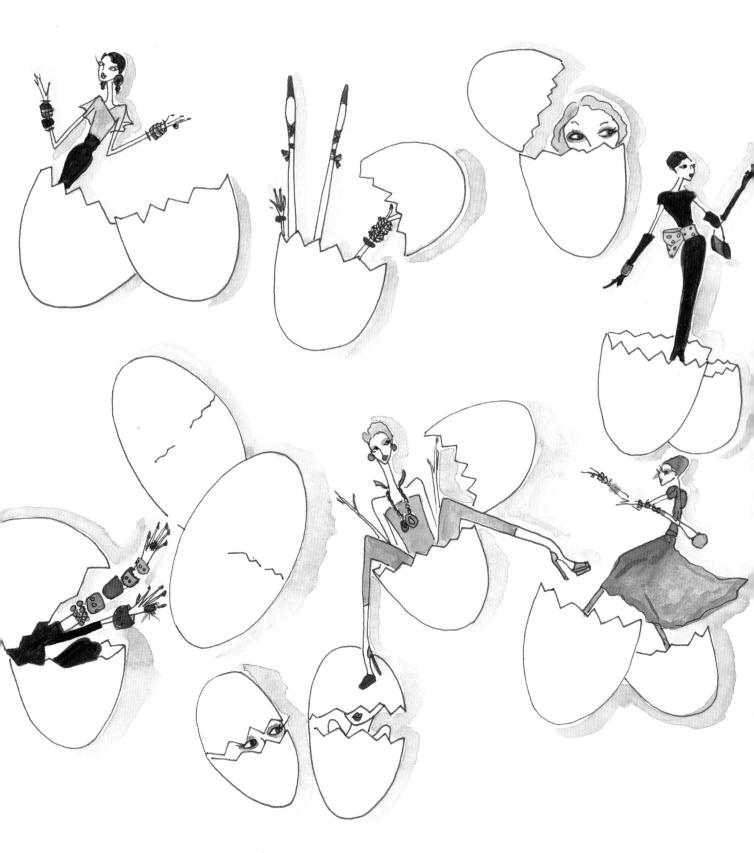

A LIFE OF STYLE | 17 |

Then, of course, there is everyone else.

Maybe we weren't lucky enough to be born with innate style.

(Innate style is like the skinny gene: you either get it or you don't.)

But we have GUT INSTINCTS that send a message to our hearts.

We are the only ones who hear it.

Sometimes we listen and sometimes,

for some ridiculous reason,

we don't.

How stupid are we when we don't listen to our gut?

I am here to say that there are no rules.

What we wear, how we live in our homes,

and how we live our lives is up to us.

There is no rule book.

We make the choices. We are our keepers.

We have our instinct buttons to rely on.

And yes, we will make mistakes.

Everyone does.

But who cares?

Live and learn.

Better yet: *live, learn, and laugh.*

We all need to laugh at ourselves every so often.

So don't be afraid to listen to your gut.

Most of the time you will be happy with the result.

There are No Rules in style, just Good instincts.

Innate Vs.

Cultivated

Does it matter?

Style is putting our own signature on the things that we wear and the way that we live.

Be brave.

Stylish people are courageous.

People who live a life of style are *passionate* about how they
communicate and live their style.
Fashion doesn't dictate to them.
They select fashion based on their style needs.
They define their own beauty,
create their own trends.
They love their imperfect nose,
the texture of their hair;
they accentuate their long legs or pale skin;
they vacation where they want to be
rather than migrate with the masses
for they know *who they are* and *what they love.*
They define personal style.
Stylish people believe in themselves,
and they are willing to take risks.
They have a huge sense of self-confidence; they maintain their
beliefs and endure any criticism of who they are.
They do not blend into a crowd …
rather they stand out from it.

...STYLE?

Style is not skin deep. *It is soul deep.*
It is our most significant form of expression.

*It is how we communicate
who we are to the world around us.*

It is a reflection of
who we are,
where we have come from,
and what we want to say to the world around us.

It is our voice.

Style can be expressed in our gestures and actions.
Giving, sharing, expressing, loving,
and creating something we feel deep inside
to the world around us is

the true spirit of style.

And the spirit of style can be shared in many ways.

We need to use the tools of style to
animate our lives and share our passions with others.

The French say *joie de vivre*—the joy of living.
Too often we go through life not appreciating our
ability to create joy around us.
We have the power to create emotions that can
leave lasting impressions.

HAIR
Certain style creatures have a signature "do"...like Elvis or Dolly.

MAKEUP
Makeup or its absence can be a strong style communicator. Sultry eyes, red lips, or totally natural.

VERBAL STYLE
Speech is one way of communicating style: signature words or phrases like "darling" or "It's just FAB," the tone of voice, a foreign accent...

GRAND GESTURES
Many people communicate their style with hand gestures, passionate movements that express so much.

FRAGRANCE
Some people like to communicate with scent—they leave their style signature long after their departure... you always want to be remembered.

ACCESSORIES
Opulent or not, accessories can communicate our style.

BODY LANGUAGE
Style can be expressed by the body: slink, swank, wiggle, strut...

How do we Communicate our style?

← There are countless ways →

Here are hundreds of them . . .

1. Handwritten notes
2. Text messages
3. Telegrams
4. Email
5. Postcards
6. Lipstick
7. Red lipstick
8. Pink lipstick
9. No lipstick
10. Lip liner
11. Lip gloss
12. Table etiquette
13. No table etiquette
14. Eyeglasses
15. Movie-star eyeglasses
16. Intellectual eyeglasses
17. Cars
18. Vintage cars
19. Expensive cars
20. Racing cars
21. Humble cars
22. No car
23. Jewels
24. Big jewels
25. Fake jewels
26. Fake and real jewels
27. Little jewels
28. No jewels
29. Hairdos
30. A big hairdo
31. Nail polish
32. Long fingernails
33. Round fingernails
34. Square fingernails
35. Tattooed fingernails
36. Fake nails
37. Wigs
38. Hair extensions
39. No hair
40. Short hair
41. Long hair
42. Curly hair
43. Straight hair
44. Wavy hair
45. A bob
46. A pixie
47. Music
48. Jazz music
49. Classical music
50. Blues music
51. Country music
52. Rock-and-roll music
53. Perfume
54. Aromatherapy oils
55. Body creams
56. Bath salts
57. No fragrance
58. Eye makeup
59. Hair gel
60. Hair spray
61. Pomade
62. Ponytails
63. Chignons
64. Shaved
65. Crew cuts
66. Afros
67. Perms
68. Smile
69. Big smile
70. Frowns
71. A wink
72. A twitch
73. A cough
74. A gesture
75. Hand movements
76. Lots of hand movements
77. Eye movements
78. Head positioning
79. Manners
80. A lack of manners
81. Politeness
82. Rudeness
83. Education
84. Gentleness
85. A caressing gesture
86. Body positioning
87. Posture
88. Good posture
89. Bad posture
90. Body language
91. Slouching
92. A limp
93. A swank
94. A wiggle
95. A laugh
96. A distinct laugh
97. A discreet laugh
98. Clearing the throat
99. A big over-the-top laugh
100. A sigh
101. Jokes
102. A sense of humor
103. Pranks
104. Philanthropy
105. Graciousness
106. Fetishes
107. Hobbies
108. Cocktails
109. Menus
110. Color usage
111. Neutral colors
112. Strange colors
113. Black color
114. White color
115. Every color
116. Schmaltz
117. Kitsch
118. Gimmicks
119. Vacations
120. Exotic vacations
121. Dangerous vacations
122. Work vacations
123. Suntan
124. No suntan
125. Fake suntan
126. Cosmetic surgery
127. Botox
128. No cosmetic surgery
129. Too much cosmetic surgery
130. Vocabulary
131. An extensive vocabulary
132. Vulgar vocabulary
133. Polite vocabulary
134. Limited vocabulary
135. Linguistically inclined
136. Accents
137. Voice tone
138. A lisp
139. A stutter
140. Friends
141. No friends
142. Social
143. Antisocial
144. Very social
145. Games
146. Playfulness
147. Toys
148. Big toys
149. Little toys
150. No toys
151. Seriousness
152. Intensiveness
153. Handwriting
154. Big handwriting
155. Small handwriting
156. Sloppy handwriting
157. Neat handwriting
158. Slanted handwriting
159. Curly handwriting
160. No handwriting
161. Typeset
162. Family crest
163. A pen
164. An important pen
165. A felt-tip pen
166. A desk
167. A big desk
168. A messy desk
169. A meticulous desk
170. Mirrors
171. Lots of mirrors
172. No mirrors
173. Lights
174. Bold lights
175. Dimmed lights
176. Candlelight
177. Chandeliers
178. Solar living
179. Restaurants
180. Beds
181. Canopy beds
182. Big beds
183. Simple beds
184. Parties
185. Big parties
186. Small intimate parties
187. Theme parties
188. Great parties
189. Dogs
190. Cats
191. Pets
192. Snakes
193. Birds
194. Fish
195. Sports
196. Basketball
197. Tennis
198. Golf
199. Water sports
200. No sports
201. Baseball
202. Football
203. Sports participant
204. Sports observer
205. Entertainment
206. Kisses
207. Hugs
208. Salutations
209. Affection
210. A lack of affection
211. Magazines
212. Newspapers
213. Loyalty
214. Dependability
215. Home scent
216. Bad home scent
217. Great home scent
218. Office scent
219. Hats
220. No hats
221. Over-the-top hats
222. Boy hats
223. Sport hats
224. Bandanas
225. Kerchiefs
226. Turbans
227. Scarves
228. Perfection
229. Obsessiveness
230. Imperfections
231. Casualness
232. Dancing
233. Ballroom dancing
234. Slow dancing
235. Disco dancing
236. Pole dancing
237. Herbs
238. Spices
239. Sweets
240. Oils
241. Photos
242. Gardens
243. Topiaries
244. Cigarettes
245. A cigarette holder
246. Vegetarians
247. Vegans
248. Writing paper
249. Personalized writing paper
250. A diary
251. An agenda
252. Briefcase
253. Luggage
254. Iconic luggage
255. Non-iconic luggage
256. Soft luggage
257. Rigid luggage
258. Beauty case
259. Trolley
260. No trolley
261. A lot of luggage
262. Little luggage
263. Shoes
264. Sexy shoes
265. Ballerina shoes
266. Loafers
267. Stilettos
268. Boots
269. Desert boots
270. Thigh-high boots
271. Go-go boots
272. Mules
273. Flip-flops
274. Iconic shoes
275. Platform shoes
276. Handbags
277. Vintage bags
278. A clutch
279. A shoulder bag
280. A rigid bag
281. No bag
282. A pouch
283. A boat
284. A sailboat
285. A motor yacht
286. A yacht
287. A super-yacht
288. A dinghy
289. Speedboat
290. Helicopter
291. Private jet
292. Economy class
293. Business class
294. Train travel
295. Cruise vacation
296. Camping vacation
297. Seaside vacation
298. Mountain vacation
299. Flea markets
300. Auction houses
301. Vintage shopping
302. Mall shopping
303. Walking
304. Running
305. Jogging
306. Horseback riding
307. Horse jumping
308. Rodeos
309. Cowboy hats
310. Cowboy boots
311. Sneakers
312. Corsets
313. Push-up bra
314. No bra
315. Garter belt
316. Negligee
317. No negligee
318. Slippers
319. Maribou slippers
320. Barefoot
321. Baths
322. Showers
323. Spa
324. Turkish baths
325. Massages
326. Acupuncture
327. Chinese medicine
328. Homeopathic medicine
329. Body scrubbing
330. Yoga
331. Meditation
332. Card playing
333. Poker
334. Gambling

335. Ballet
336. Opera
337. Broadway
338. Concerts
339. Pouty lips
340. Perked lips
341. Moles
342. Freckles
343. Scars
344. Facial hair
345. Frown lines
346. Body hair
347. No body hair
348. Tattoos
349. Body piercing
350. White sheets
351. Ruffled sheets
352. Floral sheets
353. Satin sheets
354. White bread
355. Baguette
356. Bagels
357. Croissants
358. Donuts
359. Picnics
360. Buffets
361. Sofa eating
362. Bed eating
363. Eating out
364. Fast-food dining
365. Fine dining
366. Tulips
367. Roses
368. Lilies
369. Peonies
370. Gardenias
371. Anemones
372. Calla lilies
373. Sweet peas
374. Lilies of the valley
375. Violets
376. Lavender
377. Cactus
378. Eucalyptus
379. Rosemary
380. Pizza
381. Cheese dinners
382. Eclectic tableware
383. Eclectic art
384. No art
385. Minimal architecture
386. Opulent architecture
387. Loft living
388. Apartment living
389. Cottage living
390. Beach living
391. Mountain cabin living

392. Suburban living
393. Urban living
394. Tent living
395. Recreational vehicle living
396. Country living
397. Isolated living
398. Ever-changing living
399. Poker
400. Chess
401. Checkers
402. Backgammon
403. Dominos
404. Pinochle
405. Bridge
406. Rollerblading
407. Ice skating
408. Downhill skiing
409. Cross-country skiing
410. Polo
411. Painting
412. Sketching
413. Sculpting
414. Writing
415. Poetry
416. Singing
417. Whistling
418. Humming
419. Snapping fingers
420. Reading
421. Not reading
422. Reading hard books
423. Reading e-books
424. Driving
425. Driving fast
426. Driving slow
427. Being driven
428. List maker
429. Obsessive list maker
430. Disorganized
431. Super-organized
432. Obsessively organized
433. Scattered
434. Forgetful
435. Thoughtful
436. Sport style
437. Animal print obsessed
438. Television addicted
439. Radio addicted
440. Vespa
441. Harley Davidson
442. Candy eater
443. Chocolate obsessed
444. Pasta
445. Pizza with anchovies
446. Furs
447. No furs
448. Fake furs
449. Leather

450. No leather
451. Black leather
452. White shirts
453. White tee shirts
454. White jeans
455. White style
456. Blue jeans
457. Used blue jeans
458. Torn blue jeans
459. Embellished jeans
460. Biker shorts
461. Martini shorts
462. Bermudas
463. Leggings
464. Black leggings
465. Black clothes
466. Black clothes 24/7/365
467. Colorful clothes
468. Monochromatic clothes
469. Black and white anything
470. Sneakers
471. Knee socks
472. Stand-up stockings
473. No sneakers
474. Pearls
475. Diamonds
476. Gold
477. Silver
478. Religious symbols
479. No religious symbols
480. Tai chi
481. Astrology
482. Tarot cards
483. Chanting
484. Spiritual retreats
485. Rosary beads
486. Asian objects
487. Jade
488. Figurines
489. Incense
490. Burning oils
491. Lanterns
492. Wood carvings
493. African objects
494. Indonesian textiles
495. Indian textiles
496. African textiles
497. Toile de Jouy
498. Polka dots
499. Stripes
500. Damask
501. Chintz
502. Linen
503. Taffeta
504. Velvet
505. Chiffon
506. Cashmere
507. Florals
508. Dramatic drapes

509. Tailored drapes
510. Embellished drapes
511. Sheer drapes
512. No drapes
513. Ruffled drapes
514. Tassels
515. King Louis chairs
516. King Louis mirrors
517. King Louis anything
518. Chaise longue
519. Wing chairs
520. Slipper chairs
521. Tufted anything
522. Biedermeier
523. Modern furniture
524. Stools
525. Benches
526. Upholstered banquettes
527. Accent tables
528. Coffee tables
529. Comfortable sofas
530. Uncomfortable sofas
531. Love seats
532. Conversation chairs
533. Conversationalist
534. A non-conversationalist
535. A partner desk
536. Footstools
537. Round dining table
538. Rectangular dining table
539. No dining table
540. Wall tables
541. Side chairs
542. Retro table lamps
543. Floor lamps
544. Halogen lamps
545. Birdcages
546. Birdcages with birds
547. Birdcages without birds
548. Blackberry
549. No Blackberry
550. Computer
551. No computer
552. Twitter
553. Facebook
554. No Facebook
555. Electronically social
556. Old-fashioned social
557. Charitable
558. Very charitable
559. Anonymously charitable
560. Socially charitable
561. Party hopper
562. Social butterfly
563. Antique collector
564. Flea market collector
565. Home shopper
566. An addicted shopper
567. Online shopper
568. Discount shopper

569. A gift giver
570. A big gift giver
571. Self-absorbed
572. Competitive
573. Super-competitive
574. Not competitive
575. Jealous
576. Selfless
577. Selfish
578. Accessible
579. Formal
580. Pretentious
581. Gracious
582. Careless
583. Carefree
584. High-maintenance
585. Low-maintenance
586. Complex
587. Simple
588. Intellectual
589. Spiritual
590. Non-spiritual
591. Explorer
592. Risk taker
593. Reckless
594. Extroverted
595. Introverted
596. Mysterious
597. Suspicious
598. Paranoid
599. Sentimental
600. Sensitive
601. Insensitive
602. Hot-tempered
603. Laid back
604. Perfectionist
605. Ethereal
606. Dreamer
607. Realist
608. Sexual
609. Sensual
610. Awkward
611. Clumsy
612. Graceful
613. Tailored clothes
614. Dramatic clothes
615. Romantic clothes
616. Sexy clothes
617. Understated clothes
618. Minimal clothes
619. Trendy clothes
620. Opulent clothes
621. Eclectic clothes
622. Country clothes
623. Ethnic clothes
624. Traditional clothes

625. Old World clothes
626. Elegant clothes
627. Eye shadow
628. Blue eye shadow
629. Pink eye shadow
630. Smudgy eye shadow
631. False eyelashes
632. No eye makeup
633. Colored contact lenses
634. Tweezed eyebrows
635. Thick eyebrows
636. No eyebrows
637. Pierced ears
638. Multi-pierced ears
639. Hanging earrings
640. Button earrings
641. Bejeweled earrings
642. Over-the-top earrings
643. Tiaras
644. Bracelets
645. Bangles
646. Many bangles
647. Cuffs
648. Necklaces
649. Pearl necklaces
650. Chain necklaces
651. Gold necklaces
652. Big bubble rings
653. Banded rings
654. Tiny rings
655. Knock-your-socks-off rings
656. Gloves
657. Elbow-length gloves
658. Opera gloves
659. Silk scarves
660. Iconic scarves
661. Cashmere scarves
662. Ponchos
663. Capes
664. Trench coats
665. Jean jackets
666. Motorcycle jackets
667. Fur coats
668. Fake fur coats
669. Goose down coats
670. Pencil skirts
671. Party skirts
672. Flirty skirts
673. Chinos
674. Cigarette pants
675. Trousers
676. Long skirts
677. Feminine blouses
678. Tailored shirts
679. Slinky tops
680. Sweaters

To understand the countless ways that style
can touch every aspect of our life
—from the most minute detail to the most profound—
is to understand the power we have
to create and define the way we live our life.

It is not about lifestyle but rather about ...

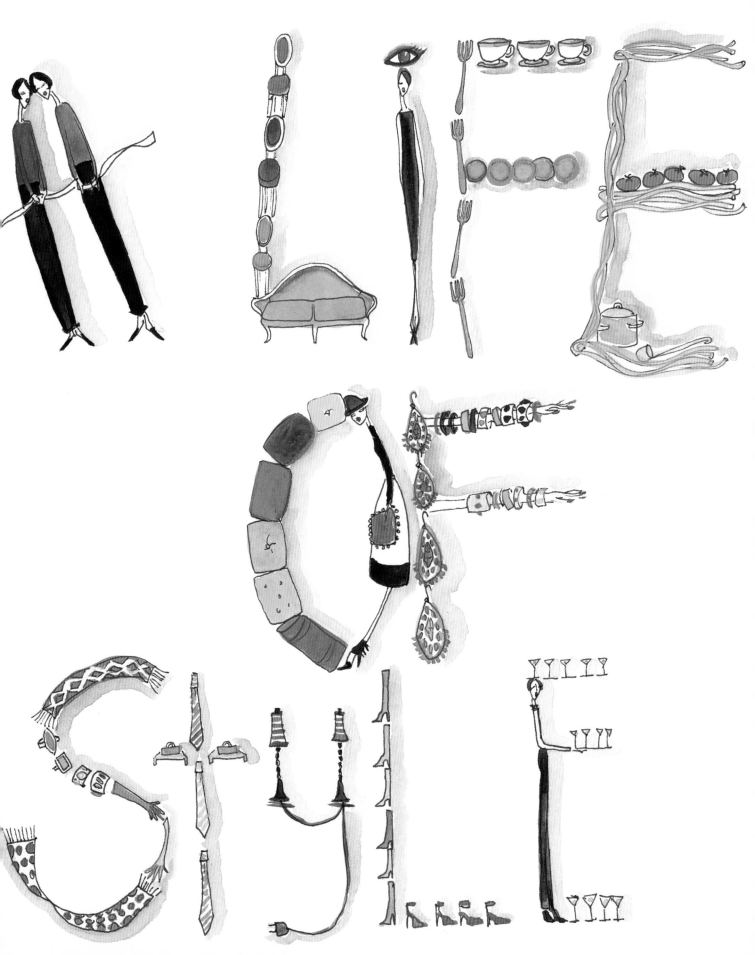

Her table centerpiece was BREAD!
can you imagine? BREAD! No flowers.
BREAD and CANDLES.

Are you joking?
It was positively divine!

Was it bad?

Went to the most stylish restaurant last night: each table had a different collection of potted herbs. It looked so charming, and the aromas... fresh herbs and candles... so romantic, what genius!

A handwritten thank you! Wow! I haven't gotten anything non-electronic in years! What beautiful paper!! custom made...

REALLY?

My kids don't even come out of their room.

Not one chair at her table matched... different styles, different colors. It was great. I went straight to the flea market and found the most adorable petite King Louis chair... I've been inspired!

Her children greeted us when we arrived. They were in the most elegant pajamas... so old world, so well mannered.

The imperfection of her look drives me mad! I WISH I could be totally imperfectly chic like that!

SALE

The table was completely black and white. After the initial shock, all I wanted to do was photograph it!

And her music mix: Mozart, Etta James, and Maurice Jarre!

What about the way her pillows were thrown around the living room?

I mean, who could wear a turban like she does?

Let's face it, it felt like a scene out of Lawrence of Arabia. I was expecting Peter O'Toole to walk in! What a dreamy night!

Style

Do I have it? Can I catch it? Can I buy it?
Where do they sell it? Does it come from Europe or can it be
purchased domestically? Is it something to be studied
or can you get it like medicine? Maybe hypnosis?
I need to understand how to have this thing called style!

Not one glass matches...
What beautiful color!
And her dress.
I wonder if she
thought this out?

How did she transform
that old broken-down sofa into
a Hollywood set? The boldness,
the color, the pillows.
Do you by chance have
a camera?

Who would ever imagine hanging
seating from a tree?
It's so *Alice in Wonderland*!

How do we cultivate our style?

OLD IDEAS

OLD AND NEW MIXING TOGETHER

NEW IDEAS — POSITIVE ENERGY

BAD VIBRATIONS

NEW INSPIRATIONS

NEGATIVE ENERGY

NEW DISCOVERIES

By opening our minds

to new ways of thinking . . .

by being honest about the things we love and don't love . . .

by being brave . . .

by getting rid of negativity . . .

by opening our eyes, hearts, and spirits to new positive thoughts . . .

by discovering and embracing our own uniqueness . . .

and by searching for inspiration.

Inspiration is

Our feel-good organs
—*the mind, the heart, and the soul*—
need inspiration
to fuel the creative voices from within.
Read, read, read . . .
books, magazines, newspapers, the Internet.
Travel. Explore.
See movies, go to the theater,
listen to music, dine, socialize,
scour flea markets and antiques fairs.

food for our spirit.

If you have ever entered a designer's studio you have
seen the inspirations that they surround themselves with.
Designers constantly search for inspiration,
motivation, stimulation, challenge.

Creative people pull from all sources—books,
theater, travel, music, art, photos, historic moments,
films, political events, wars, birth.
All of these things enter our minds and challenge
our vision and thoughts.

Inspiration makes us grow.
Grow your mind, grow your spirit,
grow your style.

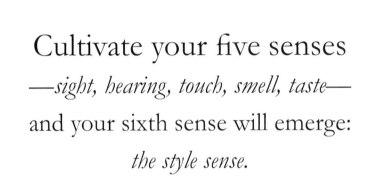

Cultivate your five senses
—*sight, hearing, touch, smell, taste*—
and your sixth sense will emerge:
the style sense.

Are you a six~sense kind of girl?

taste

touch

sight

sound

scent

WHAT IS A LOOK?

What you wear is a component of
how you want to live.
The style link goes in every direction.
Fashion, home, and living are all connected.
Your life is a "style collage."

The question you may ask is:
How do the heart and the soul enter something
that is so indulgent and superficial?

Never judge a style by its cover.

There is love and passion under all that style.
It comes from the desire to stir emotions—
BIG EMOTIONS.

A look is not about pretty or beautiful.
It's about leaving an impression . . .
a lasting impression.

What is your Style DNA?

I am a simple gal...
If you had to break down
my style DNA, I would
say I love some opulence,
for what would life be
without a bit
of grandness?

Elegance
is absolute...

Modern Elegance

Opulence

I like a bold and
defined statement.
I hate wishy-washiness...

Bold and Defined

Things must be natural—NEVER FORCED...

I need the spontaneity and romance of chic country life.

Au Natural

Country Chic

White makes me feel fresh, new, and positively creative.

And last, but certainly not least, I like it when things feel well-traveled and a bit exotic. And I like it when all of the above are tied together in an eclectic manner.

I told you, I am a simple gal.

White World

Eclectic, Exotic and Eccentric

Just give me
an eclectic mix:
a wicker
handbag, an
ikat skirt, my
grandma's fur
top, a polka dot
turban, and
some African
jewels...
I feel like
a unique kind
of gal.

I'll take a
white shirt any day.
When I feel that
crisp, clean, fresh
white shirt on my body,
I am confident and
ready to conquer.
It doesn't matter
what time it is or
where I am.
When I wear whites
and lights I feel like
a breath of fresh style.

I tend to go
a bit over the top.
"Enough" is not in
my vocabulary.
For me, it is all
about making
an entrance,
leaving an
impression—adding
some big style to
the moment. What is
life without a bit of
drama? I want
jaws to drop.

I am as black and white as they come: decisive, bold, and defined. It is or it isn't. Take a stand—a strong stand.

What is natural these days? Cashmere, materials in sumptuous shapes, a bit of the intellectual.

Country chic... floral, linens, comfort, romance... Old World charm meets garden grace.

I am all about modern elegance. I love sleek, monochromatic, sensual sophistication, never too much. It's glamour, but always in a polished manner.

She knew how to play it!

She would ski down a mountain in the
same pieces she would wear to a black tie.
Her versatility was inspiring!
It gave her the creative upper hand and
maximized her style possibilities.

Maybe she was a bit of a chameleon . . . but she had a fabulous consistency.
And consistency needs a sense of order.
How would she keep such style in order?
What was her dressing room like?

It was a playground!

A meticulous, organized playground.

With order like this you could understand how she achieved her look.

She knew what she loved, and she knew how to pull it together.

Racks were her biggest power tool—rolling garment racks.

Four of them. *She racked it all!*

Not even one closet!

She shared with me the quintessential rules of her personal style.

"Every gal needs a look.

To get a look you need clarity.

For clarity you need order.

This is my order:

Three racks for my fundamentals,

whites, naturals, and darks …

then a fourth rack—the WOW rack,

that ever-changing, ever-evolving mood ring of style.

The pieces on my racks are those that I absolutely, positively LIVE IN.

Those are the pieces that are the most comfortable

and have the most versatility.

They are the confidence pieces.

Sweaters, scarves, stockings, shoes, hats …

everything else goes on my accessory table.

Simple, no?

Don't forget everything starts from color.

Color rules it all."

Color is a mood communicator.

Color can soothe,

it can WOW,

it can seduce,

it can empower . . .

it puts the mood into motion.

Whether fashion, cosmetics, accessories,

or objects for the home,

my starting point is always color.

Color is simply the most powerful element in my design process.

I choose color thinking about not just the singular effect

but the power it has against all other colors, textures,

and elements.

The most exciting part of working with color

is to push the partnership of unexpected marriages.

This is how you create new energy for the eye.

Color can reinvigorate,

create a sense of optimism,

renew just about anything,

and in particular,

stir our emotions.

This is what I always say about color.

1. Choose what you absolutely LOVE.

2. Never let it match your eye makeup.

3. There are NO rules.

Color will tell everyone how you feel.

It is a MOOD INDICATOR.

Be careful what you reveal.

Playing the Color Cards

To makeup or not to makeup?

Makeup is a tool of style.
It can create a mood, an emotion;
it can hide, it can enhance,
it can evolve as we evolve.
It can say what we want or hide what we choose . . .
as can its absence.
My mother always said,
"Never leave home without your face!"

A face doesn't have to be in full drag . . .
it just needs something to give you a look.

A red mouth makes them read your lips.
Manicured hands let them know
you are high maintenance.
Smoky eyes hypnotize.
And blush on the cheeks makes it clear
you're not just sleeping in the bedroom.

What's Perfection?

Perfect? Imperfect? Who's to say?
When it comes to defining beauty,
we need to embrace uniqueness.
Our crooked nose, frizzy hair, wide-set eyes:
these form a powerful signature of style.
Remember: It's the imperfections that make the charm.

*When I was a kid everyone
made fun of my lips.
Now my girlfriends ask their cosmetic
surgeons to copy them!*

When I was twelve years old,
my Aunt Sadie told me that I would be
much cuter if I had my nose done.
Now I'm twenty-four. I didn't have it done,
but I am done with my Aunt Sadie!

I have always had
a BUTT...
and when I was in high
school the boys used to
say, "What are you
serving today?"
now—thank you J.Lo—
when I walk into a room,
I stop and look over
my shoulder to see the
eyes on me and
my you-know-what
and say, "BUT what is
your name?" The guys
always smile.

In grade school the kids
used to call me pinhead!
well yes, my head is much
smaller than my body,
and my ears do stand out,
and I have a mole the size
of a dime on my cheek,
but I just got the cover
of French Vogue!
Who's laughing now?

Don't Rely on Money

IN STYLE WE TRUST

WHERE THERE IS A STYLE WILL THERE IS A STYLE WAY

Developing your style is

NOT ABOUT MONEY.

It is about the desire to get an effect.

Great style makers mix the disposable

with the luxurious.

Don't be a snob.

With the power of the Internet,

fashion, lifestyle trends,

and information

are up for grabs.

You can get the desired effect at every

price and quality.

The art is in choosing well.

How does she get such a chic look on her salary? Maybe she comes from money. I've got to ask my boss for a raise!

Does she know my dress cost $89? And that my earrings are flea market finds?

Is it strange that I spent more on these shoes than on my new sofa? And the dress cost me $129. Is something out of whack here?

If the question is, Do I spend $59 or $450?, then there's nothing to discuss. My style carries $59 just fabulously!

She often wore her
most precious jewels with her most amazing bijoux.
*No one could tell
what was what.*
They assumed it was all REAL.
People believe what they want to believe.

It's all about ownership.

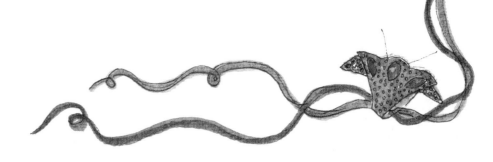

Passion or

Obsession?

What is it about women and shoes?
Whether obsession or passion,
it is a most common fetish.

If my soul had a body
part it would be
my feet. And I love
to nurture my soul!
(I wonder if that's why
the bottom of the shoe
is called the sole.)

Why shoes?
I always feel thinner
with new beautiful shoes.

Bijoux, bags, bandanas,
belts, bangles, berets, and brooches—
these are the toys of style!
These magical touches
can transform your look
in a flash.

Whether it is the "it" accessory of today
or a magnificent trinket of years gone by,
an accessory can
illuminate, regenerate, and re-create.
Think of a great accessory collection
as a treasure chest that any style pirate
would love to dig up!

What does a handbag say about us?

Do we carry it in hand or on a folded arm (like the queen)?

Or do we shoulder it?

Is it an envelope that we caress?

Iconic or ironic?

Status symbol or just the contrary . . .

understated, unmarked, and undetailed?

Is it bejeweled or positively simple?

Does a small bag mean we have little or we carry little?

Do we need a mega-bag to shout who we are?

Does our bag
empower us
or do we
empower ourselves?

The Queen of Versatility

What she could do with a scarf!
Each of her tools of style had multiple purposes.
She had a vision and she didn't care if anyone knew
her elegant stole was the sofa throw!
She knew how to make her favorite things go the distance ...
Once she wore a vintage napkin as an ascot.
It was quite divine!

The Gardener of Style

Did her garden inspire her fashion or
did her fashion
inspire her garden?

Scent

Scent can send a bad mood running.

Fragrance will linger long after we are gone.

It amazes me how much memory is attached to scent.
Petals, herbs, fruits, and spices are just a few of the elements
that bring about a heightened sense of smell.
Whether it is a personal fragrance, a candle, or a meal,
a scent can change and define the mood
for ourselves and others.

Our scent choices affect how we
see our world, bringing us that much closer to
defining our style.

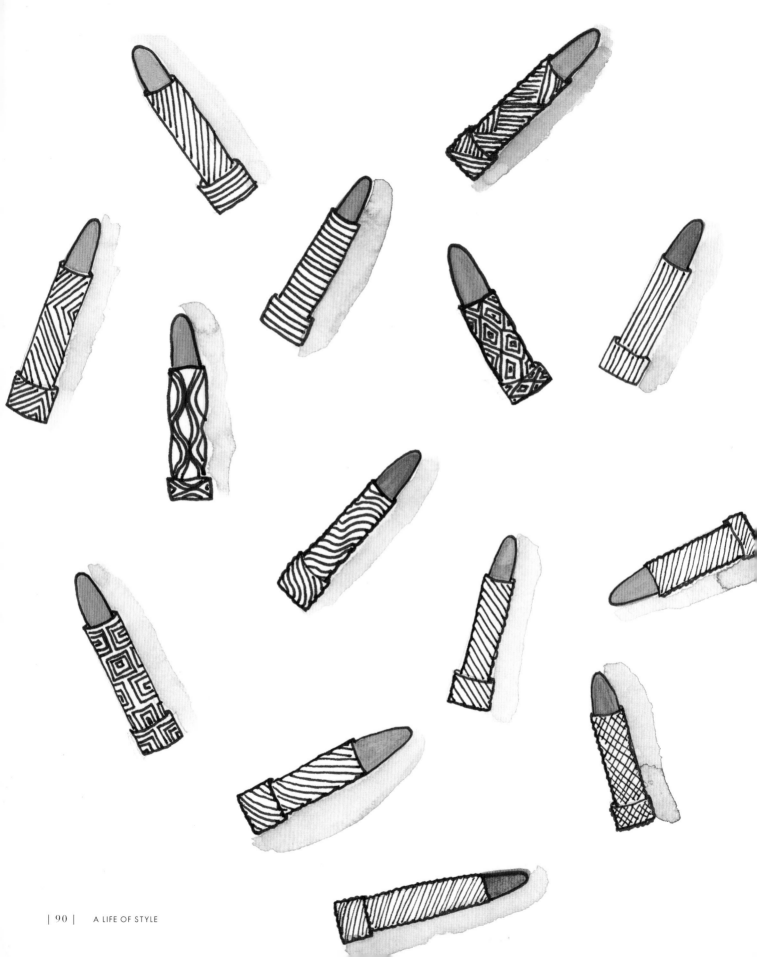

Your signature is not always written in ink ...

Mannerisms, expressions, posture,
body language all *animate our style.*
Clothes are a tool of style. But don't forget:
We wear our clothes—they don't wear us.

Why is it that what we see isn't
always what we feel?
Baggage.
We all have it.
If we can get rid of those subliminal suitcases,
we can find the courage to do what we want to do
and live the style we so desire.

WHAT DEFINES A HOME?

Some people say home is where the heart is.

I say home is where there is

heart,

soul, and style.

Creating a home is

creating a world of your own.

The Foyer

First impressions say a lot.

What is the first sensation when someone enters?

What does the entrance say—or not say?

Is there a "feel good" feeling?

With a foyer like this, you better believe there is.

The checkerboard floor, the delicious pink paint and striped wallpaper

—how bold and courageous,

how happy—

the beautiful fresh flowers, the burning candles,

the settee with colorful tufted pillows,

the stacks of beautiful books on the side bench,

the picture frames filled with memorable moments ...

and what of the aromas arriving from beyond?

Nothing seems to match and yet everything works together.

It wasn't how she put her furniture together; it was how her furniture brought people together.

She could take a hallway and turn it into a room of its own.

Her colors...
how do they work in
such harmony?

Books say it all . . .

She was a twenty-first-century girl
with an eighteenth-century bedroom.

Bedrooms are rooms for dreaming.

Her bed was totally Hollywood— tailored glamour, even when she slept.

She was a swinger in the bedroom.

Make room for spirituality.

Spirituality is about believing, aspiring, searching for awareness.
Whatever form of spirituality you believe in, it is about nurturing your
heart and soul—*understanding yourself from the inside out.*
Carve out a space to nurture your soul.

Spirituality is the soul of style.

The Bathroom

Is your bathroom a private oasis?

A place to relax, de-stress, reflect?

Surround yourself with things you love:

colors that soothe,

lighting that is easy on the eyes,

aromatherapy candles,

beautiful towels, robes, and slippers.

Your bathroom is your world.

Make it feel good

and it will make you feel good.

The Kitchen

Unexpected elements
can give even the tiniest of kitchens a
BIG personality.
Table lamps,
crystal chandeliers,
sofas, eclectic chairs,
skirted tables,
great color,
and patterned wallpaper *(washable, of course)*
along with some amazing elements
of contrast convert a
utilitarian room into
a *style definer*.

King Louis reigns.

It doesn't matter if the chair is an antique or a copy.

(Well, yes, a real King Louis would be fabulous,

but there is no reason not to live the dream!)

Real or fake is not the issue.

Great design is great design.

And King Louis is great.

King Louis anything

—chair, table, pouf, mirrors—

a touch of opulence makes for a rich life.

The wonderful thing about King Louis is that

with fabulous material and a little lacquer

you can make magic.

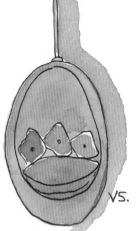

VS.

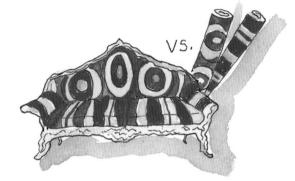
VS.

VS.

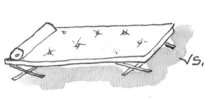
VS.

VS.

VS.

VS.

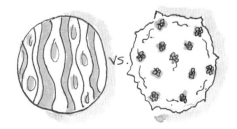
VS.

What could be more fascinating than
a King Louis chair with a Knoll marble table?
A Chinese chest with a 1960s egg chair?
An opulent crystal chandelier with a yellow-lacquered Parsons dining table?
Unusual style marriages rarely end in divorce.

Need a lift?

There are so many ways to lift your style.
A seductive red lipstick,
a manicure,
or a new pillow for the sofa:
these are the tricks,
the fast and affordable ways
to make something tantalizingly new,
to reinvent yourself.

purple pleated lampshade, stilettos, or bangles... so uplifting!

Pillows are like jewelry—you can never have enough.

Don't forget turbans, tiaras, and teacups.

Style Constants

King Louis Anything

Mini King Louis

A Writing Table

A Wing chair ...old intellectual charm...

...Pillows... Pillows... and more Pillows.......

The Pouf

Unusual Lamps and Shades

Books ...cerebral style

Exotica ... Symbols of a Well Traveled Life .....

Screens... the mystery and tease element...

A chaise longue

Mirror, mirror on the Wall.....
Think gilded, grand and
gorgeous!

Stripes & toiles in wallpaper, fabrics, tablecloths,
and anything it can be applied to......

Perfume for the Home

A Divinely Comfortable Sofa

accent tables to show your passions

The Feelgood Throw

The Angled Banquette

Crystal Candlesticks

Charming Slipper Chairs ...and "mini" Slipper Chairs

Flowers and Unusual Vases...

Important Drapes...

Botanical Life

Kitsch Anything

Crystal Chandelier

Eclectic Wall Hangings
Gilded Mirror

Colorful Side Chair

Wall Sconce

Unusual Colored Glass Lamps

"objects"

Vases

The Modern Element

Stools

The Great Wall Table Scene

Framed Photos

The Bench

How do you dress your furniture?

Upholstery is like dressing.

It's not just putting a piece of fabric on a chair or a sofa ...

the finest details have to be examined.

How does the chair feel inside: is it comfortable?

Does it make you want to melt into it with your favorite book?

Does it make you want to cuddle with someone you care about?

Will the fabric wear well?

Is it a showpiece or a piece you want to live in?

Should it be tailored or romantic?

Elegant or rustic?

Simple or embellished?

Colored strongly or detailed subtly?

Should it blend or should it pop?

Tassels or pompoms?

Ruffles or scalloped hem?

Piped seams or topstitched?

Removable, like our clothes, or fixed?

Would Marie Antoinette approve?

When living in a Marie Antoinette state of mind
you can't help but dream of ruffles, bows, tassels—
the most embellished trim you can imagine.
"Decoration" is an understatement.
There are no boundaries, just good starting points.

Whether you are designing a ruffled cover
for a favorite slipper chair, preparing a soufflé
Grand Marnier, or designing a ball skirt that
would make even Scarlett O'Hara jealous, just think,

What would Marie do?

Tassel and braids will swing your style into high gear.
These Old World upholstery adornments are unique accessories, making of each piece of furniture a jewel.
Each one is a piece of craftsmanship . . . unique, individual, and very highly styled.

How do we make a dramatic statement
and still keep it modern?
We need to study the past to understand the future.
And what about the present?
Our style is a reflection of how we live today.
Our style journey is always in motion.

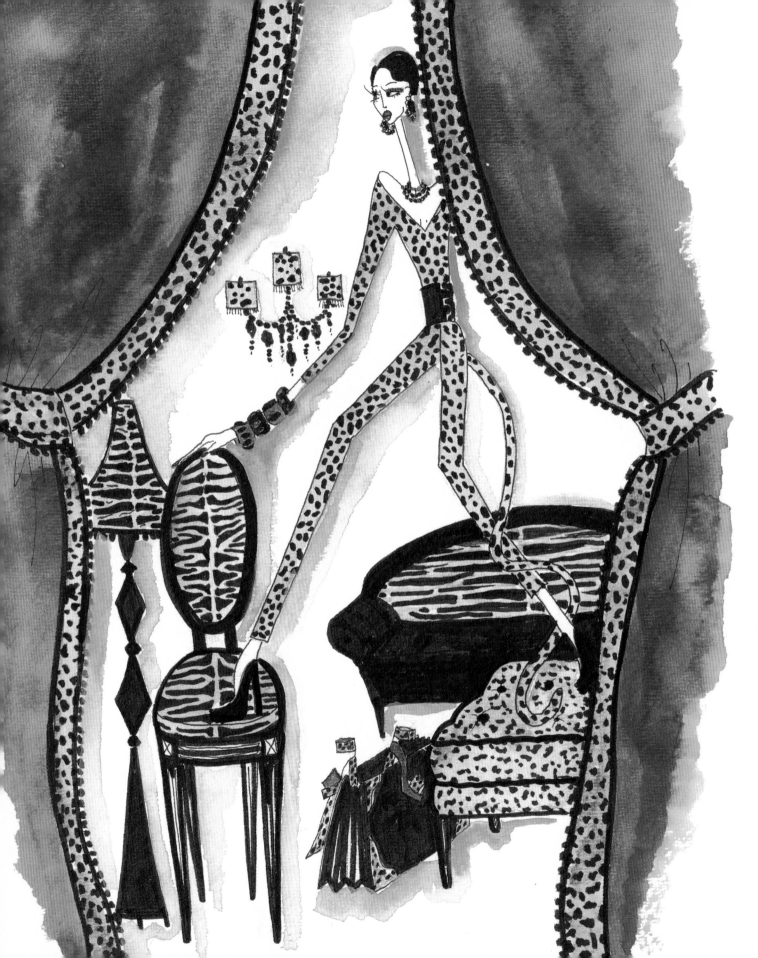

THERE'S A LITTLE Jane in ALL of US

What is it with these savage markings that so many of us crave?

Whether a sofa, stiletto, corset, or cushion,

these beasty signatures say a lot about what we feel.

Are we telling the world that we have a savage streak?

Maybe a sexual voice bursting to emerge?

Is it some Hollywood glamour that will add a bit of zest

to our otherwise blasé life?

Perhaps we are truly craving a bit of the wild?

She was part Marie Antoinette, part Indian princess,
part Chinese empress, part Jane, and part Mata Hari.
She was a character out of an exotic Hollywood movie. She was a citizen of the
world—she could have been from anywhere ...
so exotic, so well traveled, so belonging not to
one place but to every place.
This was her style.

Her home was like a journey.
Leopard, jade, ikats, and lacquer;
quilts and Fu lions;
wicker and carved-wood sculptures;
Maasai beading, kimonos, and Kashmir shawls;
King Louis and Le Corbusier.
What a marvelous MIX of things she loved!
The blend is what gives a sense of authenticity to style.

Remember, *it's all in the mix*.

good Morning

夜平暑挽

Style Fetishes.... Obsession or passion???

Paris

Quirky, Kitsch Passion

Cuff Obsessed

Rick Obsessed

Superstition Obsessed

Heart Passion

Foot Passion

Writing Passion

Sea Passion

Eye Passion

Rose Obsessed

Coin Obsessed

Cheese Obsessed

CHURCHILL QUOTES

Literary Passion

Hat Passion

Time Obsessed

Ball Passion

Does it matter? In Life we need to live with Passion!

Table Obsessed

1 teaspoon of Passion

Flickering Passion

Vase Passion

Horn Passion

Glove Passion

Lip Passion

Style fetishes are those amazingly passionate objects
that we can't live without.
Sometimes the objects are things we showcase
and sometimes they are held in very private collections.

Art Passion

Jane obsessed

Wine Passion

Cut crystal … regal reflections …
it must be the princess syndrome!
I feel like a princess when I have a chandelier.
When I look at a chandelier,
I think of jewelry—in particular, earrings.
What a great earring it would make!
Crystal chandeliers have the ability to fit in anywhere.
I am always amazed how a chandelier suits any
environment—even an outdoor garden!
I also love to have a chandelier in the kitchen.
What unexpected contrast!
With its transparency and reflection,
a chandelier becomes a neutral glamour element.
(And don't forget about crystal wall sconces!)

Crystal
Chandeliers

How do we light our life?

Lamps: you can never have enough.

They add charm, uniqueness, and style to any environment.

There are two equally exciting elements—

the lamp itself and the lampshade.

Oh, the shades!

Don't think they have to match.

Imagine the pleated effects, the pagoda shapes, the printed organzas ...

Besides the design impact, a great lamp creates a warm glow.

When a room has a golden glow, everyone in it glows.

A window or a movie set?

Remember Scarlett in *Gone with the Window*—
ooh, I mean *Wind!*
Just imagine wearing those drapes …

She was a dreamer and a writer. She gazed at her rose garden while pruning her thoughts.

With her collection of vintage magazines on her big, flower-filled table, she had all the inspiration she needed to get her style mojo going.

Was it the chanting or the celestial-blue-velvet chaise longue that soothed her soul?

The " I Want to be Alone" Curtain

The Kitchen Cabinet Curtain

The Back Stair Curtain

Curtains aren't only for windows.

The Sink Curtain

They can create closets, add privacy to a space, divide a room,
hide what needs to be hidden.
Drapes project a certain glamour and drama.
Beautiful fabric adds an element of texture
and design that builds an individual statement.
Think about a bold stripe framing an arched doorway with
beautiful passementerie and a fringed hem.
It's the details that define great style.

Intellectual Space

Set aside a bit of intellectual space.

When you grow your mind, you grow your style

from the inside out.

Her yellow Mozart room
brought her clarity at the
end of the day... and a gift of
music to anyone who passed by.

Some people speak,

and others write.

These are the DESK-SETTERS.

The STYLE they use is what makes them

individual.

Where they write is as individual

as what they write.

What they write is as private or as public as

they choose.

How they write tells you everything,

right down to their soul.

ARE YOU A DESK-SETTER?

LOUNGE DESK
There are those who need to recline for literary moments...

HIDDEN DESK
A true desk-setter is resourceful.

BATHROOM DESK
For writers who crave PRIVACY.

ROOM DESK

Putting pen to paper is one of the most cherished forms of communication.

PIN-UP WALL DESK

Some desk-setters need frontal inspiration: memos, reminders, and enough post-its to fill a wall...

PARTNER DESK

A lifetime partnership needs a lifetime partner desk.

Style Dictators

Wallpaper is a style dictator, just like red lipstick.

(If you apply red lips, say goodbye to all other makeup.

The lips will rule.)

Wallpaper is definitive.

A person who chooses wallpaper

is a person who really knows her style.

It is much more of a statement than paint.

Paint changes and evolves;

wallpaper is absolute.

If you use a wallpaper, you must do it with WOW!

Knock your socks off!

When you make a statement, make it memorable!

Mirror, mirror on the wall, who's the most stylish of them all?

Why, the gilded ones, of course.

a tiny meek space

When blessed with a tiny space,
BE COURAGEOUS!
Turn it into a POWER space.
Strong color,
daring wallpaper,
sparkling chandeliers,
and bold prints
animate your world
with a space that has a life of its own.

A POWER SPACE

She grew up
in a Southern
Baptist church,
and so her hats were as important
as her prayers. Her mama's and
grandma's collections of millinery were
more than hats to her. They were
memories and symbols of her heritage.

Her Sicilian great-aunt
cherished hand-woven
linens, all personally
monogrammed by her
great-grandmother.
Her favorite niece knew
there was no present
more majestic than this
glorious linen towel
collection.

Ever since she
was five years old,
she had loved her
grandma's
leopard stools.
She used to
sit on them
and have her
warm cookies
and hot chocolate.
Thirty years later,
the stools are front
and center in her
foyer for all to see.

Her name was MacDougal,
and she loved being part of a true
Scottish clan. Her family tartan
was her signature. Even though
she and her twin sister were
twenty-first-century cyber-girls,
when it came to important
correspondence, it was all on the
family-crested paper.

Style Traditions

Defined and attached to her style was
an obsession with genealogy. She mounted and
framed three generations of black-and-white photos.
When people entered her world,
they saw what was important to her.

Style traditions
might be heirlooms,
generations of family DNA
passed down.
Or they might be
treasures of history
that signal our origins,
sometimes predictable
and sometimes not ...

Her mother had the most magnificent collection of
1930s deco dishes: Clarice Cliff, Susie Cooper, and Shelley ...
Each dish had a memory, a piece of her mother's taste and style—
something she wanted to make a part of her own style.

It seems that people crave
BIGGER AND BIGGER
and
GRANDER AND GRANDER.
But there is something quite fabulous
about living a life of
Petite Charm.

Small can be an enchanting form of high style.
Less can be better—
less cost, less complication.
You can play the power cards in a small space:
brilliant color, vibrant wallpaper, strong window treatments.
By doing so, you make a minute space powerful:
compact, comfortable, and chic.

1. Bold blue-striped curtains
2. A very high library
3. Pottery
4. The perfect leopard slipper chair
5. Green velvet banquette
6. A red-lacquered wedding armoire
7. Colorful tufted pillows
8. Black-framed etchings with colorful mats
9. Unusual lamps and shades
10. A simple door with contrast molding
11. Sconces
12. The open kitchen
13. Dishes on wall
14. One wallpapered wall
15. Wall table
16. Stationery
17. Red-lacquered folding tables
18. A fabulous sofa (with bed)
19. Slipcovered bench
20. Tassel
21. A window seat
22. A red wall
23. Bordered area carpets
24. Red-lacquered floors
25. Two side chairs…a dinner for four?

If you looked into the windows of
this house what would you see?

You would see a life lived.

When you enter, you can't help but

FEEL GOOD.

It is so intoxicating that the hostess is nicknamed

Mrs. Feel Good.

When people come to her home,

they leave feeling good.

HOW ARE MEMORIES MADE?

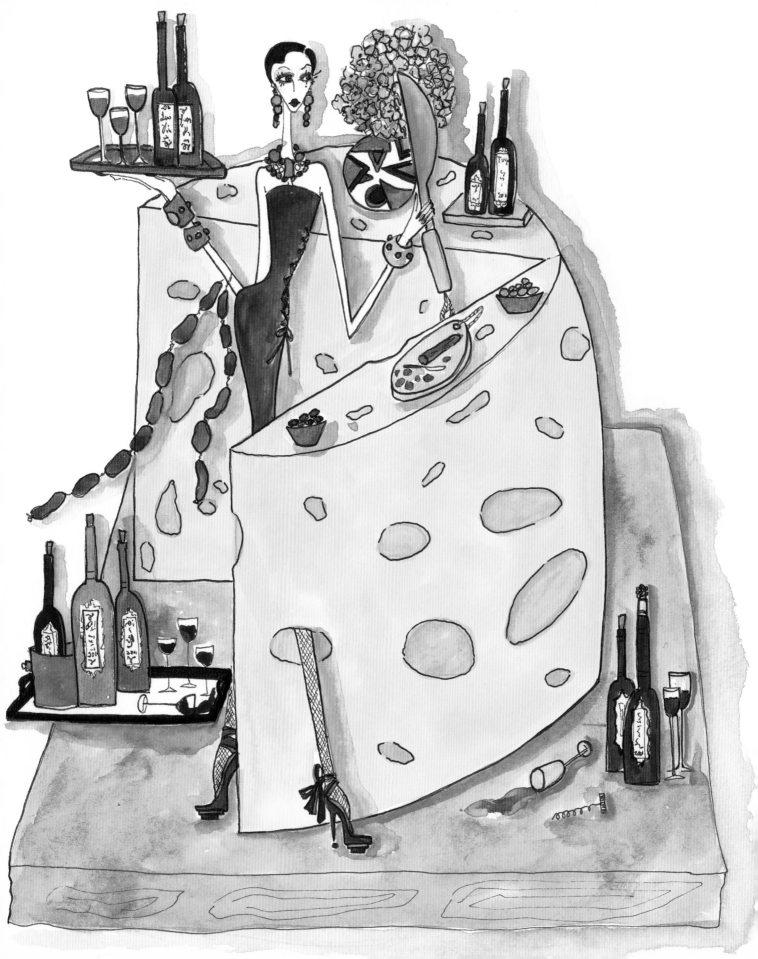

A remarkable hostess is remarkable
not because she knows how to make a cocktail
or cook a memorable meal
or style the most unforgettable table
but because she knows
how to bring people together.

Life should be celebrated each and every day.
There are no second chances.
Use the tools of style to make your home
a playground of life's best moments.
It doesn't matter whether it is Tuesday night
or Saturday night,
dinner with the kids
or a cocktail with friends.
Each day can be a memorable event—
and *why not?*

She always began with the "list."
(And what a list it was!)
You could say she was the
Queen of Lists.
Real style is in the details.
And it is the fine details
that her guests would remember,
whether a rose encased in
an ice cube or
her signature red anemones.
With pen in hand
she conquered the world,
point by point,
check by check.

When making a guest list,
think of it as cooking the most original,
the most intriguing meal.
Each guest is like
a flavor . . . a spice . . . a texture.
Each has a special quality;
together they can create an imperfectly delicious mix.
The mix is EVERYTHING!

Add one well-spoken
couturier.
Mix in two raconteurs.
Fold in one
complete stranger.
Sprinkle with world
travelers
and
glib intellectuals.
Let simmer.

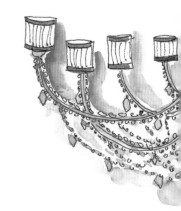

When you create magic at your table,

they don't just remember the table—

they remember you!

1. Don't "set" the table, "dress" it. The choice of table linens comes first.

2. Think of the center of the table as the stage. Captivate your guests with a bit of theater.

3. A unique charger gives a foundation to each place setting.

4. Choose a beautiful mix of dishes.

5. And don't forget the flatware. Stick to one pattern or mix and match.

6. The napkins can be detailed, almost as though each is a little scarf.
   wrap a special herb, like rosemary, or a single rose inside.

   7. Crystal makes every beverage taste better.

8. Remember the finishing touches: silver bread dishes, beautifully written place cards,
   a few rose petals.

Destiny or

To seat or not to seat?

Seating is a strategic step in making

any meal work its charm.

Who are the talkers?

The wits?

The conversationalists?

The storytellers?

Contrast is important.

Decided

And it's always fun to toss in a mystery guest.
I love adding an unknown element . . .
Sometimes it's better to have an approach in mind—
decided seating is controlled.
And sometimes it's great to play the wild card—
let destiny take its course . . .
Is your seating destiny or decided?

Mixing your dish patterns is as important as mixing your dinner guests.

Call me Vanilla.
If you're into scent,
gorgeous color,
and exotic silhouette,
then I'm your girl.

I'm Maia.
My flower is lily
of the valley.
If you're searching
for a return
to happiness,
I'm the flower for you.

My name is Tulipa.
I am grace and
elegance; my body
moves like a dancer
taking a pose.

Hey there, I'm Violet.
I'm a sentimental girl,
delicate and tender.
Romance is my name,
and faithfulness
my game.

Hi, my name is
Dahlia. I'm a bit of
a wild card:
colorful, feisty,
and eclectic.

Your flowers reflect you.

Or is it the other way around?

Each flower has a message,

each petal has an emotion,

each fragrance reveals

a secret aspect of your mood.

Music can transform a mood faster
than any drug.
All of your carefully selected visual elements
will go flat without a strong soundtrack.
Sunday brunch needs a playlist that will encourage
your guests to take time with their coffee.
The cocktail collection should relax them.
And then there are the dinner mixes, the after-dinner mixes,
and the after-after-dinner mixes . . .
Always keep your ears open
and stay in tune with great sounds.

You are what you serve.

Think of your home as a Hollywood set.

You are the Director of Ambience.

Think about the special effects,

characters,

mood,

lights—

every detail from the very big to the very small.

You have a captive audience

that needs to be

charmed,

relaxed—

thoroughly entertained.

Do you know what style buttons to push?

Are you ready to become the Fellini of home entertaining?

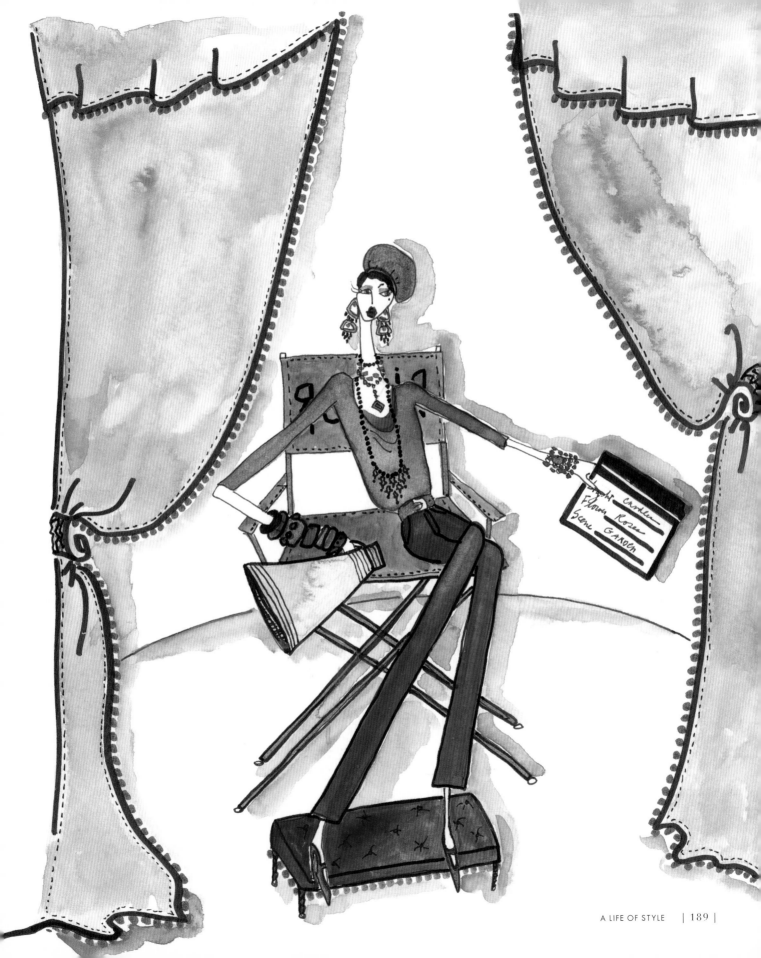

A pineapple in one hand and a martini in the other.

What better way to greet a guest?

MY ONLY RULE:

Upon arrival, all worries must be left

in my green-lacquered

Worry Box.

When you entertain,

you are inviting people into your world.

You want them to leave their worries at the door.

But how?

Think the *six* senses.

Seduce them with warm aromas,

a delightful soundtrack,

tasteful appetizers,

and interesting company.

Cocktails anyone?

Cocktails are a grown-up thing,
and she loved dressing like a grown-up—
cocktail dress, turban, sexy shoes, and of course,
all the bijoux you can imagine.

What is it about martinis that
make them as chic
as a little black dress?

It is the most chic,

forever stylish cocktail.

But have some other classics up your sleeve:

a Manhattan,

an Americano,

a champagne or Campari cocktail.

And for brunch, *always* Bellinis.

Your guests will get in the mood

before they can blink!

I love to collect the most beautiful crystal stemware, *old and new.*
And I don't use my crystal just for special occasions.
Beer or diet soda—everything tastes better in crystal!

She was raised to deal with crisis situations,
so when a dinner for four
became a dinner for eight,
she didn't fret.
She created two tables side by side
and started a game of
lottery seating.
Each guest picked a number out of a hat—
it was a wild-card party!

After dinner is the time to decamp to the living room
for tempting sweet delicacies,
like marrons glacés and chocolate bonbons.
Your guests will forget their diets.
Grappa and cognac, unusual teas and coffees,
a wonderful collection of tea cups:
every detail is pure style.
(Don't forget to change the music.)

A LIFE OF STYLE

I know a party is a true success
when at 2:00AM someone shouts,
Butta la pasta!
Translation: Put the pasta on!
This is called La Spaghettata di Mezzanotte.
It doesn't taste quite the same at
any other hour of the day.
You need to be relaxed, passionate,
uninhibited.
La Spaghettata di Mezzanotte
is *soul spaghetti.*

When the last guest leaves,
I sometimes notice that my green-lacquered
Worry Box is still full.
The guests left their worries at the door
and forgot to pick them up!
The best gift of all is the gift of relaxation
and great pleasure.

DEFINE YOUR LOVES

True style is understanding who we are and having the conviction to express it.

BE BRAVE

Stylish people are courageous.

RELY ON YOUR INSTINCTS

There are no rules in style, just good instincts.

GET PASSIONATE

We need to use the tools of style to animate our lives and share our passions.

SEARCH FOR INSPIRATION

Inspiration makes us grow. Grow your mind, grow your spirit, grow your style.

DON'T RELY ON MONEY

The art is in choosing well.

DEVELOP THE SIXTH SENSE

Cultivate all five senses—sight, hearing, touch, taste, smell— and then your sixth sense will emerge: the style sense.

MIX IT, DON'T MATCH IT

The mix is what makes the look and mood real.
Opening our minds to a world of contrast is essential.

EMBRACE IMPERFECTION

It's the imperfections that make the charm.
Develop your uniqueness as a powerful signature.

COMMUNICATE WITH COLOR

Color is a mood communicator.
It is a powerful insight into how we feel and what we love.

CULTIVATE VERSATILITY

Versatility gives you the creative upper hand.

THE COMFORT FACTOR

Comfort motivates security; security motivates style.

DO AS YOU DREAM

If you don't like the way you live, change the way you live.

The Monacelli Press and the M design are registered trademarks of Random House, Inc.

Library of Congress Cataloging-in-Publication Data
Moses, Rebecca.
A life of style : fashion, home, entertaining / Rebecca Moses. — 1st ed.
p.   cm.
ISBN 978-1-58093-293-6
1. Fashion. 2. Beauty, Personal. 3. Entertaining. I. Title. II. Title: Fashion, home, entertaining.
TT507.M715   2010
746.9'2—dc22   2010018589

Printed in China

www.monacellipress.com

10 9 8 7 6 5 4 3 2 1
First edition

Designed by Moses Media